Things to Make for Your Doll

KATHY ROSS

ILLUSTRATED BY ELAINE GARVIN

THE MILLBROOK PRESS
Brookfield, Connecticut

To my sweetest little doll, Julianna

Library of Congress Cataloging-in-Publication Data
Ross, Kathy (Katharine Reynolds), 1948–
Things to make for your doll / Kathy Ross; illustrated by Elaine Garvin.
p. cm.
Summary: Presents twenty projects for making clothing and accessories for dolls, including a bathing suit and beach bag, jewelry, bulletin board, and clothes closet.
ISBN 0-7613-2861-0 (lib. bdg.) — ISBN 0-7613-1781-3 (pbk.)
1. Doll clothes—Juvenile literature. 2. Dress accessories—Juvenile literature. 3. Doll furniture—Juvenile literature. [1. Dress accessories. 2. Doll clothes. 3. Doll furniture. 4. Handicraft. 5. Sewing.]
I. Garvin, Elaine, ill. II. Title.
TT175.7.R667 2003   745.592'21—dc21   2002153492

Published by The Millbrook Press, Inc.
2 Old New Milford Road
Brookfield, Connecticut 06804
www.millbrookpress.com

Printed in the United States of America
5 4 3 2 1 (lib.)
5 4 3 2 1 (pbk.)

Contents

Don't toss out your doll's odd socks! Use them to make your doll her very own sock puppets.

Doll Sock Puppets

Here is what you need:

felt scraps

doll sock

small wiggle eyes

small pom-poms

scissors

white craft glue

yarn

Here is what you do:

1. First you will need to decide what kind of puppet you want to make for your doll. It could be a person puppet or some kind of animal.

Rabbit? ? ? ? ? Duck ? ? Frog ? ? ? Mom ? Dad? ? ? ?

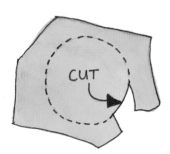

2. Cut a 1-inch (2.5-cm) circle for the mouth of the puppet from felt.

3. Turn the toe end of the sock in about ½ inch (1.25 cm) to form a puppet mouth. Glue the felt circle inside the mouth.

4. Glue the two wiggle eyes above the mouth.

5. Use a small pom-pom for the nose of the puppet or cut a nose from felt.

6. Add details to the puppet such as yarn hair for a person puppet or long ears cut from felt for a rabbit.

ADD GLUE

Making sock puppets for your doll is just like making sock puppets from your own old socks. Use your imagination and creativity to come up with lots of different puppet designs.

RABBIT

MOM

DUCK

DAD

Slip a puppet over each hand of your doll and help her put on a puppet show. What fun!

Capture the handprint of your special doll friend in plaster.

My Doll's Handprint in Plaster

Here is what you need:

plaster of Paris

one or more 2-inch (5-cm) jar lids

disposable plastic tub and craft stick for mixing

plastic wrap

poster paints and a paintbrush

paper clips

water and paper towels for cleanup

newspaper to work on

Here is what you do:

1. Take your doll's pretty clothes off so you do not get any plaster on them. Cover the doll's hand with plastic wrap.

2. Mix some plaster in the disposable container following the instructions on the package.

3. Fill a lid with plaster for each handprint you are making. It's a good idea to make several and then save the best ones.

4. Press the doll's plastic-covered hand into the wet plaster. Because dolls' hands are often curved and do not move, you may not be able to get a print of the entire hand. This is not a problem. Get as much of the shape of the hand as you can, then use the craft stick to carefully dig out the rest of the hand shape. (If you use a slightly larger lid for one of the handprints, you will have room to put your doll's name under the print. You can make the letters with a pencil point.)

5. Slip one end of a paper clip in the plaster at the top of the handprint to make a hanger.

6. Let the plaster dry hard overnight.

7. Paint the plaster handprint one or more pretty colors.

BACK OF LID WITH FELT

You might want to try using a loop of ribbon glued to the back for a hanger. You can also display the handprint on a table. If you do this, glue a circle of felt to the back of the lid to keep it from scratching the table surface.

A tisket, a tasket, make your doll a basket!

Circle Basket

Here is what you need:

uncoated white paper plate

markers or crayons

white craft glue

thin craft ribbon

two 6-inch (15-cm) pipe cleaners of different colors

scissors

tiny hole-punch

tiny stickers

Here is what you do:

1. Cut the rim off the paper plate.

RIM

2. Use the markers or crayons to color both sides of the center part cut from the plate.

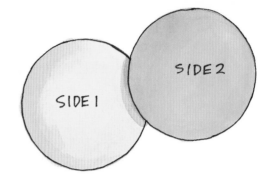

SIDE 1

SIDE 2

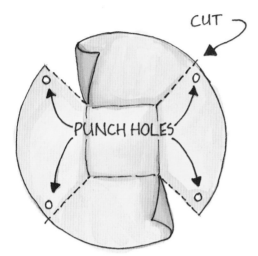

CUT

PUNCH HOLES

3. Cut four 1¾-inch (4.5-cm) slits, spacing them evenly around the circle.

4. The circle should now have four sections. Punch a hole on each side of one of the sections. Do the same with the section directly across from that one.

5. Cut a 6-inch (15-cm) piece of ribbon. Thread the ribbon through the hole on one side of each flap.

6. Pull the sides of the two flaps together over the flap between them, by tying the ribbon into a bow.

THREAD

7. Do the same thing on the opposite side of the basket.

CONTINUED ON NEXT PAGE

9

8. Twist the two pipe cleaners together to form a handle for the basket.

HANDLE INSIDE BASKET

9. Glue an end of the handle to the inside of two opposite sides of the basket.

10. Decorate the outside of the basket with some tiny stickers.

Baskets are useful for all sorts of things. They are great for collecting small flowers, jellybean eggs, or seashells, or just for storing things like doll puppets, mittens, or jewelry. You might want to make your doll several different baskets. To make a larger basket cut a larger circle from light cardboard or construction paper.

Discarded socks are perfect for making quick and easy doll clothes. Try this idea!

Sock Bathing Suit and Beach Bag

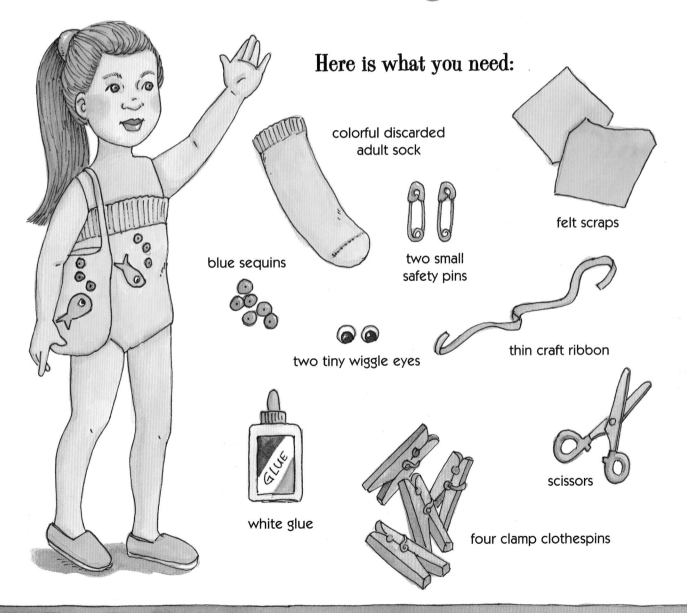

Here is what you need:

colorful discarded adult sock

felt scraps

blue sequins

two small safety pins

two tiny wiggle eyes

thin craft ribbon

white glue

four clamp clothespins

scissors

Here is what you do:

1. Cut the top part of the sock off the foot end. The top part will become the bathing suit.

2. Try the cuff on your doll. If it seems too long for a bathing suit trim the cut end off. It should be about 6 inches (15 cm) long.

3. Use the safety pin to hold the front and back of the center of the cut end together to make the crotch of the bathing suit.

4. Cut a 2-inch (5-cm) fish shape from the felt scrap.

5. Glue the fish to the front of the bathing suit.

6. Glue the wiggle eye to the head of the fish.

7. Glue three blue sequins coming up out of the fish's mouth to look like bubbles.

8. Cut a 5-inch (13-cm) -long piece from the toe end of the sock to make a beach bag.

9. Cut a 1-inch (2.5-cm) slit on each side of the bag.

CUT

INSIDE OF BATHING SUIT

TURN SOCK INSIDE OUT FOR PINNING

5"

1-INCH SLIT

10. Fold the top of the bag over on each side and glue the edges to secure the fold. Use clothespins to hold the fold in place while the glue dries.

11. Cut a 2-foot (60-cm) length of ribbon.

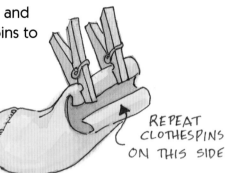

REPEAT CLOTHESPINS ON THIS SIDE

12. Pin a safety pin to one end of the ribbon.

13. Work the pin through the folded top of the beach bag to pull the ribbon through the folded edges to make a drawstring top.

TRIM IF NEEDED

14. Knot the two ends of the ribbon together at a length that is good for your doll and trim off any excess ribbon.

15. Cut a thin band from the remaining foot of the sock to use as a hair scrunchie.

What other outfits can you make for your doll using socks? How about a new skirt or a sundress?

Make a balloon for your doll that really "floats."

Floating Balloon

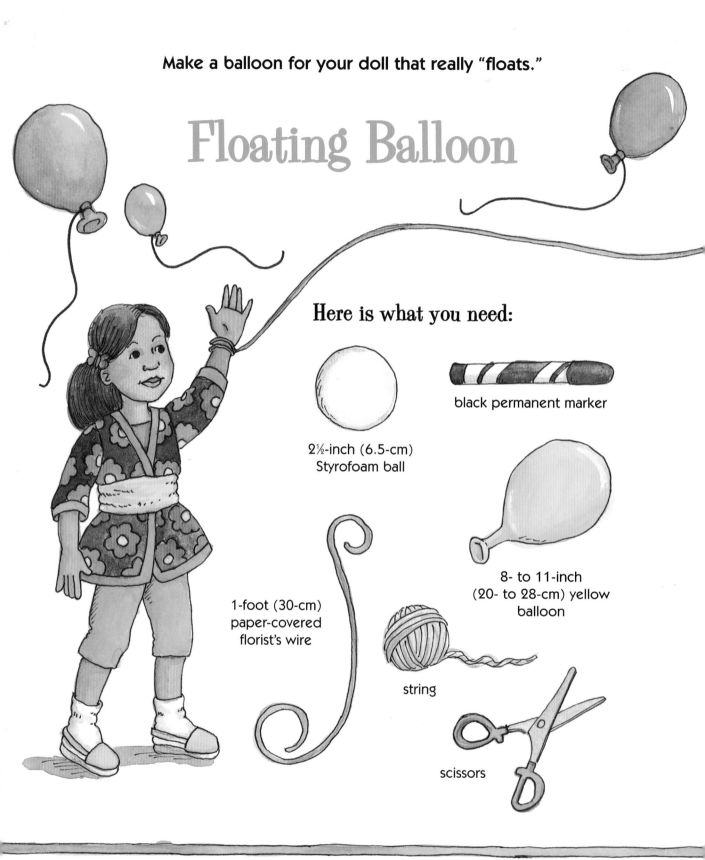

Here is what you need:

2½-inch (6.5-cm) Styrofoam ball

black permanent marker

1-foot (30-cm) paper-covered florist's wire

string

8- to 11-inch (20- to 28-cm) yellow balloon

scissors

Here is what you do:

1. Cut the neck off the balloon.

2. Cover the Styrofoam ball by pushing it into the balloon.

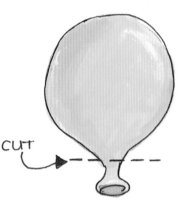

cut

3. Push one end of the florist's wire through the opening of the balloon and into the Styrofoam ball.

4. Tie the opening of the balloon shut over the Styrofoam ball and around the wire with a piece of string.

5. Use the marker to give the yellow balloon a smiley face.

6. Wrap the other end of the wire around your doll's hand so that the stiff wire supports the "balloon" to make it look like it is floating.

Your doll will probably want lots of balloons in different colors.

I think every doll should have a pet! Don't you think so, too?

Aquarium and Hermit Crab

Here is what you need:

clear plastic blister pack, such as the kind batteries come in

small seashell or medium macaroni shell

plastic milk cap

sand

twine

two tiny wiggle eyes

green tissue paper

white craft glue

GLUE

scissors

Here is what you do:

1. Trim the edges from the blister pack so that you are left with a straight-sided container to use as an aquarium for the hermit crab.

2. Cover the bottom of the aquarium with glue. Sprinkle the glue with sand. Let the glue dry before putting anything else in the aquarium.

SPREAD GLUE AROUND USING YOUR FINGER TIP

USE A SPOON TO SPRINKLE SAND

3. Put the milk cap, topside down, in the bottom of the aquarium for a water dish for the crab.

4. Tear some bits of green tissue to look like lettuce. Put the tissue lettuce in the aquarium to provide food for the hermit crab.

5. Cut two 1-inch (2.5-cm) pieces of twine for the legs of the crab.

6. Glue the twine legs in the opening of the shell so that they are sticking out.

7. Glue the two wiggle eyes in the opening of the shell, just above the legs.

8. Place the hermit crab in the aquarium.

Hermit crabs make such nice quiet pets!

If you are going to make your doll some new clothes, you might want to make a nice closet to put them in.

Box Doll Closet

Here is what you need:

cardboard carton about 12 inches by 18 inches (30 by 46 cm) and at least 10 inches (25 cm) deep

¼-inch (0.75-cm) wooden dowel

scissors

two 1-inch (2.5-cm) wooden beads

white craft glue

newspaper to work on

craft paints and paintbrush

Here is what you do:

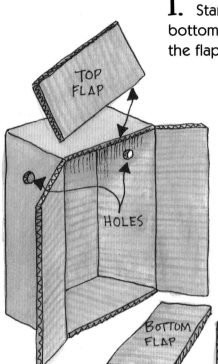

1. Stand the box on one of the short sides so that the bottom of the box becomes the back of the closet and the flaps on each side become the doors of the closet. Cut off the flaps at the top and at the bottom of the carton and save them to use for making the bulletin board on page 24.

2. Poke a hole for the dowel in each side of the closet about halfway back and about 3 inches (8 cm) down from the top.

3. Slide the dowel in through one of the holes and out through the other hole to make the clothes bar.

4. Trim the dowel so that about 1 inch (2.5 cm) of dowel sticks out on each side of the closet.

5. Glue a wooden bead over each end of the dowel to secure it.

TOP FLAP

HOLES

BOTTOM FLAP

CONTINUED ON NEXT PAGE

6. Paint the closet one or more colors both inside and outside. Or you can line the inside of the closet with pretty paper instead of painting it.

7. Decorate the closet using stickers, cut-out pictures, paint stamps, pretty trims, or whatever else you can think of to make it look nice. Decorating is definitely the most fun!

If you want the closet doors to stay securely shut, insert a paper fastener through the inside edge of each door to look like a doorknob. To hold the doors shut tie a piece of thin craft ribbon around the two fasteners, then tie the ribbon in a bow.

IMAGES TO TRACE, COLOR AND PASTE ON YOUR NEW DOLL CLOSET

Make your doll her very own scrapbook.

Padded Cover
Doll Scrapbook

Here is what you need:

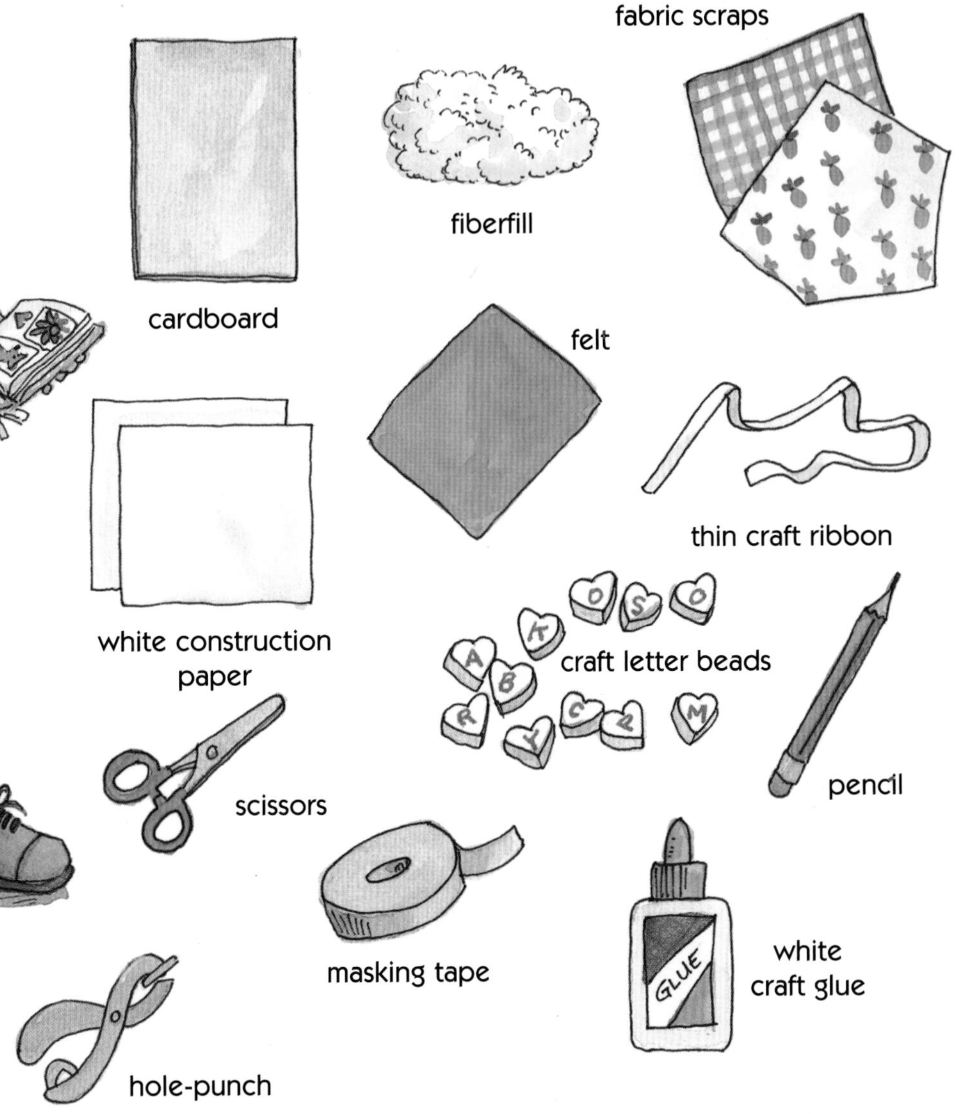

fabric scraps

cardboard

fiberfill

felt

white construction
paper

thin craft ribbon

craft letter beads

pencil

scissors

masking tape

white
craft glue

hole-punch

Here is what you do:

1. Cut two 5- by 3 ½-inch (13- by 9-cm) pieces of cardboard for the front and back covers of the scrapbook.

2. Punch two holes, 2 inches (5 cm) apart, along one short side of each cover so that the book can be tied together.

3. Glue a thin layer of fiberfill to the outside of the front cover. Make sure you do not cover the holes with fiberfill.

4. Wrap the front cover with pretty fabric, using masking tape to secure the edges on the back.

CARDBOARD
FIBER FILL

WRONG SIDE OF FABRIC FACING UP TOWARD FIBER FILL

FABRIC

5. Cover the taped side of the cover by gluing on a rectangle of felt.

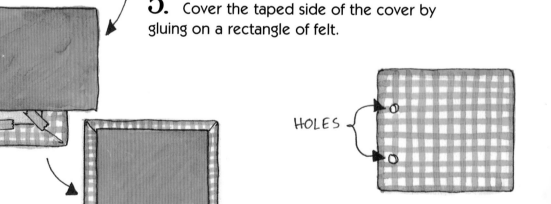

HOLES

6. Punch holes through the fabric to match the holes under the fabric in the edge of the cover.

7. Make the back cover in the same way as the front cover.

8. Cut six 5- by 3½-inch (13- by 9-cm) construction paper pages for the inside of the scrapbook. Use the pencil to mark the edge of the top page where the holes are punched in the covers.

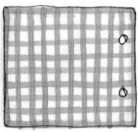

BACK COVER   FRONT COVER

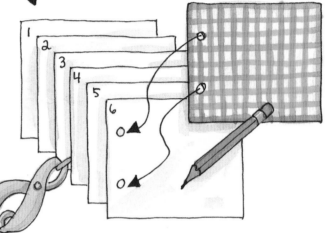

9. Punch two holes through the edge of the papers.

10. Put the papers between the front and back covers of the scrapbook.

11. Thread a piece of thin ribbon through the holes and tie it in the front in a pretty bow to hold the book together.

12. Use the craft letter beads to write something on the front of the book like your doll's name or "My Scrapbook."

Use paper scraps and small pictures and stickers to decorate the pages in your doll's scrapbook. To find "photographs" of your doll and her friends to put in the book, cut pictures from a catalog of your doll or a similar doll. You can also go to doll sites on-line and print out pictures.

Help your doll to get organized with this nifty bulletin board.

Doll Bulletin Board

Here is what you need:

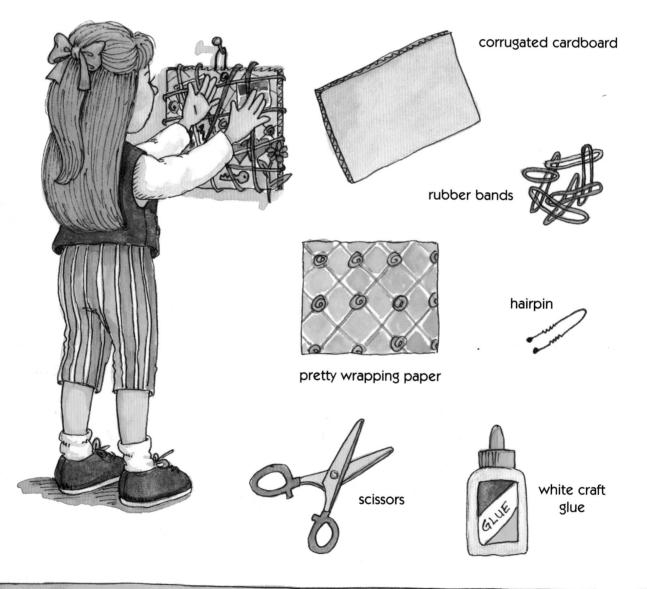

corrugated cardboard

rubber bands

pretty wrapping paper

hairpin

scissors

white craft glue

GLUE

Here is what you do:

1. Cut an 8- by 8-inch (20-cm) square of corrugated box cardboard.

2. Cut an 8- by 8-inch (20-cm) square of the pretty wrapping paper.

3. Glue the wrapping paper to one side of the cardboard square to cover it.

4. Dip the ends of the hairpin in glue and slide them partway into the holes in the center of one side of the cardboard so that the top of the hairpin forms a hanger for the board.

5. Put several rubber bands around the board in different places and at different angles to form a criss-cross pattern of elastic over the bulletin board.

Tuck little pictures, flowers, notes, and homemade greeting cards behind the rubber bands to attach items to the board.

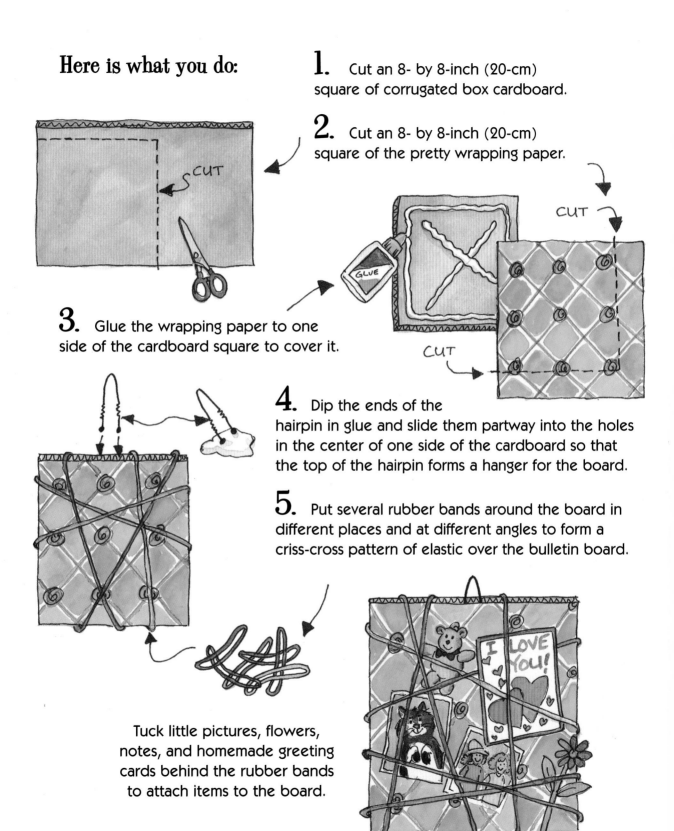

Try this idea for making pretty hangers to use in your doll's new closet.

Craft Stick Hanger

Here is what you need:

three wooden tongue depressor sticks

cup hook

white craft glue

craft paints and a paintbrush

thin craft ribbon

newspaper to work on

scissors

clamp clothespins

Styrofoam tray for drying

Here is what you do:

1. Cut one of the wooden sticks in half.

2. Use the scissors to trim away a tiny amount on each side of the cut stick.

3. Glue the two pieces of the cut stick on top of a second stick.

4. Glue the screw-end of the cup hook in the small space in the center of the cut stick to form a hook for the hanger.

CUT AWAY SPACE IS IN CENTER

5. Glue the third stick over the cut stick and the screw-end of the cup hook.

6. Secure the three sticks with clamp clothespins and place on the Styrofoam tray to dry.

7. When the glue has dried, remove the clothespins.

8. Paint the wooden part of the hanger with craft paints.

AQUA PAINT

9. Use the craft ribbon to tie a tiny bow to glue at the base of the hanger hook.

Make lots of different color hangers with different trims and decorations on them.

Discarded wrapping paper is just what you need to make
a collection of colorful hats for your doll.

Wrapping Paper Hat

Here is what you need:

wrapping paper—plain or in pattern of your choice

thin craft ribbon

two rubber bands

tiny artificial flowers

stapler

white craft glue

scissors

plastic wrap

Here is what you do:

1. Make 2 identical circles of wrapping paper. The size will depend on how large a brim you want on the hat. Begin with an 8-inch (20-cm) diameter circle.

2. Cover the plain side of one of the pieces with lots of glue. Lay the plain side of the other side onto the glue. The edges do not need to match exactly because they will be trimmed.

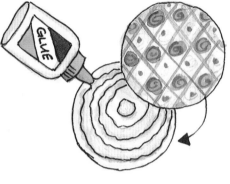

3. Put a square of plastic wrap over your doll's head for protection and secure it with a rubber band.

4. Shape the center of the glued paper over the top of your doll's head to form the hat. Hold in place with the second rubber band. Bend the edges out to create a brim.

5. Carefully trim around the edges to create an even brim for the hat.

6. Let the glue dry to set the shape of the hat. You can do this by leaving it on the plastic covered doll or by carefully removing it and setting it on a flat surface to dry undisturbed.

7. Trim the hat by stapling a pretty ribbon around it. Tuck some flowers in the ribbon on one side and secure with glue.

8. Take the plastic wrap off your doll once the gluey hat has been removed.

Create a whole wardrobe of hats for your doll in different prints and colors.

Make a paper bag mask for your doll.

Bag Elephant Mask

Here is what you need:

brown lunch bag

scissors

stapler

pencil

Here is what you do:

1. Flatten the bag so that you can cut through both the front and the back at the same time.

2. Leaving a strip up the middle about 1 inch wide (2.5 cm), cut a rectangle out of each side of the bag.

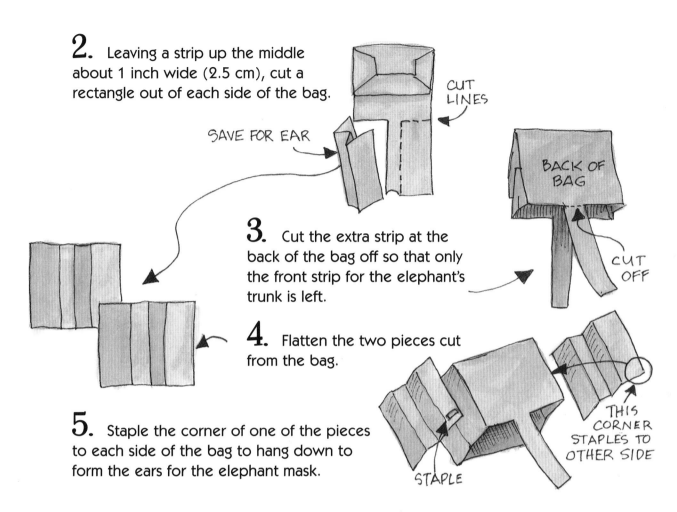

SAVE FOR EAR

CUT LINES

BACK OF BAG

CUT OFF

3. Cut the extra strip at the back of the bag off so that only the front strip for the elephant's trunk is left.

4. Flatten the two pieces cut from the bag.

5. Staple the corner of one of the pieces to each side of the bag to hang down to form the ears for the elephant mask.

STAPLE

THIS CORNER STAPLES TO OTHER SIDE

6. Put the bag mask over your doll's head to determine where the eyeholes need to be. Mark the area of each eye lightly with the pencil.

7. Cut the eyeholes in the front of the mask.

You can make a matching elephant mask for yourself by following these instructions using a grocery bag. Try making bag masks of other animals for you and your doll.

Make a little jewelry box for your doll to keep all her new jewelry in.

Doll's Jewelry Box

Here is what you need:

cardboard
toothpick box

felt

fabric that
looks nice with
the felt

trim

craft jewel
or old earring
jewel

clamp clothespins

white
craft glue

scissors

Here is what you do:

1. Carefully unglue the box and flatten it.

2. If the box has side flaps, trim them off.

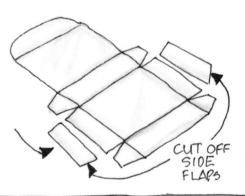

CUT OFF
SIDE
FLAPS

INSIDE
OF BOX

TRIM
AWAY FABRIC

3. Glue the inside of the box to a piece of fabric, print side of the fabric out.

4. Trim off the excess fabric around the edges of the box.

5. Glue the outside of the box to a piece of felt.

6. Trim the felt leaving a ½-inch (1.25-cm) edge around the box.

7. Fold the flattened box back into a box. This will stretch the felt some.

8. Glue the box in place, using clamp clothespins to secure it until the glue is dry.

9. Fold the flap of the box in and glue it in place, securing the fold with clothespins.

10. Trim off the excess felt around the edges.

11. Decorate the outside of the box with trim and a craft jewel in the center of the lid.

What an attractive way to store your doll's jewelry when she isn't wearing it.

Here are some ideas for making jewelry for your doll.

Doll Jewelry

Here is what you need:

cardboard tube

embroidery floss

markers

sticky-back Velcro™

thin organdy ribbon

pony beads

scissors

paper-covered florist's wire

craft gems

white craft glue

small hole-punch

Here is what you do:

Bracelet

1. To make a bracelet for your doll, cut a ring 1/2-inch (1.25-cm) wide from the cardboard tube.

1/2 INCH

2. Cut the ring open and trim it to fit around your doll's wrist without slipping off.

CUT & TRIM

3. Punch a tiny hole in each end of the cardboard strip.

4. Color the strip with markers.

5. Put a dab of glue on the inside of each end of the bracelet in order to secure the beginning of the floss.

6. Anchoring the end of the floss in the glue dab, wrap the strip with embroidery floss to cover it, beginning after the hole punched in one end and stopping when you reach the hole at the other end. Anchor the end with another dab of glue.

7. Using another color floss, wrap a second layer, widely spaced, over the first to decorate the bracelet. Again, anchor both ends with glue.

8. Cut two 6-inch (15-cm) pieces of floss. Tie an end of a floss piece through each hole to make ties for the bracelet. This will allow you to easily secure the bracelet on your doll's wrist. To remove it, just untie the ties.

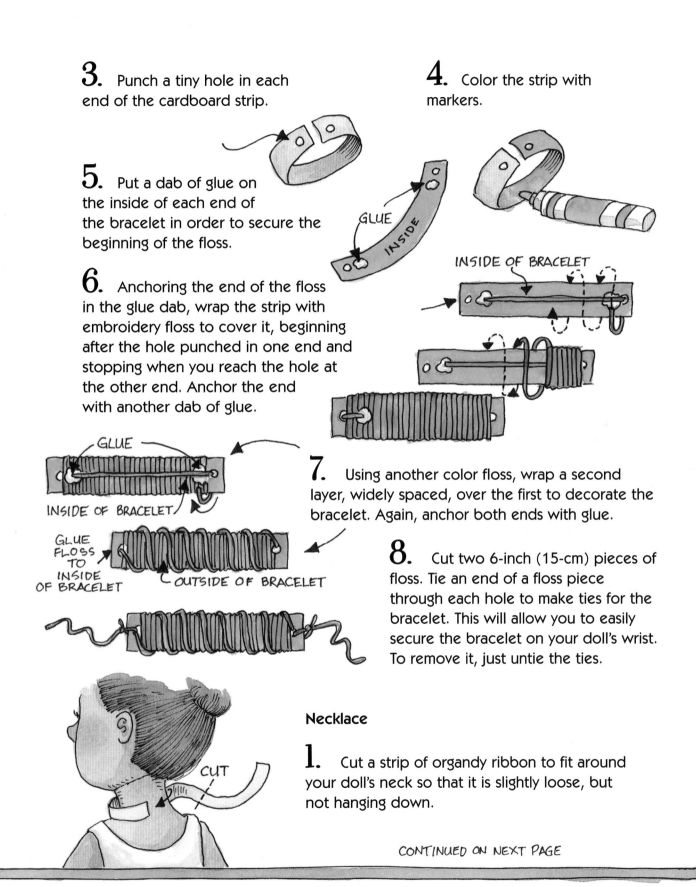

Necklace

1. Cut a strip of organdy ribbon to fit around your doll's neck so that it is slightly loose, but not hanging down.

CONTINUED ON NEXT PAGE

2. String pony beads on the ribbon, leaving space between them. If they slide around too much, secure them with a dab of glue.

DAB OF GLUE

OUTSIDE OF NECKLACE

INSIDE OF NECKLACE

3. Glue a tiny piece of Velcro to the ends of the ribbon for a fastener.

Ring

1. Cut a tiny piece of paper-covered florist's wire to wrap around your doll's finger for a ring.

2. Glue a tiny craft jewel on the front of the ring.

CUT

How pretty!

USE BEADS IN DIFFERENT SIZES & COLORS WITH OTHER RIBBONS FOR THE NECKLACE

YOU CAN GLUE TINY BEADS BETWEEN THE SECOND COLOR OF FLOSS

USE DIFFERENT COLORED & SHAPED GEM STONES OR

THREAD TWO SMALL BEADS ON FLORIST WIRE & GLUE IN PLACE

A stretchy glove can be turned into mittens and ear warmers for your doll friend.

Mittens and Ear Warmers

Here is what you need:

stretchy glove

pretty trim, ribbon, or sewing decoration

scissors

white craft glue

Here is what you do:

1. Cut a 2-inch (5-cm) piece from two fingers of the glove to make the mittens.

2. Glue a pretty decoration to the wrist of the glove. Use only a dot of glue so that you do not interfere with the ability of the glove to stretch.

CUT

3. Cut the wristband off the glove for ear warmers without cutting the band apart.

CUT

4. Use a dot of glue to attach a pretty decoration to the top of the band.

These mittens and ear warmers are so quick and easy you can make your doll several different sets in no time. Maybe your doll has a friend she would like to give a set to as a gift.

What doll wouldn't like a tray of cookies and lemonade?

Doll Treats

Here is what you need:

3½-inch (9-cm) metal jar lid

two flip-top rings

felt

large yellow pom-pom

film or small pill canister, white or clear

clear glitter

trim or rickrack

Flex-Straw

½-inch (1.25-cm) buttons

glue

red craft paint and small paintbrush

white craft glue

masking tape

seed beads

scissors

Styrofoam tray to work on

Here is what you do:

Glass of Lemonade

1. Make a doll drink by putting the yellow pom-pom in the plastic canister to look like lemonade.

2. Cut a 3-inch (8-cm) piece off the top of the straw.

CUT

3. Slip the piece into the doll glass so that the straw bends at the top of the glass.

Pink-Frosted Cookies

1. Squeeze a small amount of glue onto the Styrofoam tray.

2. Tint the glue pink with a drop of the red paint. Use the paintbrush to mix it into the glue.

RED PAINT

3. Paint the top of three or four buttons with the pink glue to look like frosting. Sprinkle the button cookies with clear glitter (sugar) or seed beads (sprinkles).

YUM!

CONTINUED ON NEXT PAGE

Snack Tray

1. Turn the jar lid top-side down to become a tray for the snacks.

2. Cut a circle of felt to glue on the top of the tray, inside the lid.

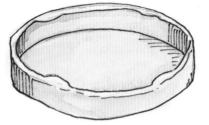

CUTTING HINT: USE THE JAR LID TO
TRACE A CIRCLE
... THEN CUT THE FELT CIRCLE
A LITTLE BIT SMALLER

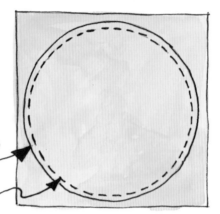

3. Glue the flip-top rings to opposite sides of the bottom of the tray so that they will stick out on each side to form handles for the tray. Secure the glued rings with a strip of masking tape.

4. Cut another circle of felt to glue on the bottom of the tray, covering the taped edges of the handles.

5. Glue trim or rickrack around the edge of the tray.

My doll is able to hold this tray by slipping the rings over her thumbs. Maybe your doll can carry the tray, too.

Here is a great idea for making costumes for your doll.

Un-Stuffed Animal Costume

Here is what you need:

old stuffed animal slightly taller than your doll (the animal must be all one piece)

scissors

sticky-back Velcro

plastic grocery bag

Here is what you do:

1. Cut a slit down the entire back of the body of the stuffed animal.

2. Remove all the stuffing from the stuffed animal. Put the stuffing in the plastic bag and save it to use for other craft projects.

CUT SLIT HERE

3. Cut a slit the width of the front of the head of the animal under the mouth.

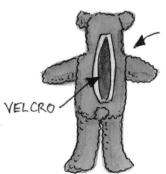

VELCRO

4. Put Velcro dots or a strip of Velcro down each side of the cut in the back of the animal so that it will close.

Put the animal suit on your doll with the head of the doll peeking out through the cut under the mouth. Check garage sales for old stuffed animals to use for making doll costumes.

**Make this beautiful headpiece so you can play
"let's pretend" with your doll.**

Fairy Crown

Here is what you need:

thin craft ribbon in three
or more pastel colors

paper covered
florist's wire (pipe
cleaner or regular wire
would work, too)

tissue paper
in pink and
purple shades

scissors

yellow embroidery
floss

white craft glue

Here is what you do:

1. Shape the wire into a ring
that fits on your doll's head.
Secure the ring by wrapping the
wire around itself.

CUT

TIE KNOTS TO
START &
FINISH

2. Cover the wire ring by wrapping it
around and around with ribbon. Tie off the ends of the ribbon at the beginning
and at the end, leaving an 8-inch (20-cm) piece, or longer, hanging down on

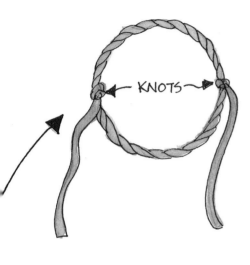

opposite sides of the ring. You may need to use more than one length of ribbon to cover the ring.

3. Tie additional 16-inch (40-cm) lengths of ribbon on each side of the ring. By tying each piece so that the two ends are equal, you will get two 8-inch (20-cm) ribbons hanging down for each piece you cut. Six to eight ribbons hanging down on each side looks very pretty.

TIE ADDITIONAL RIBBONS AS A GROUP (NOT ONE AT A TIME)

4. Cut four 1 ½-inch (4-cm) circles from the different color tissue papers.

5. Cut a 1-inch (2.5-cm) piece of yellow floss for each circle.

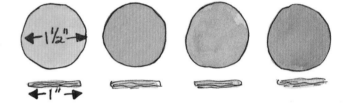

GLUE

6. To make each flower, pinch the center of the circle together with the yellow floss sticking up to form the stamen found at the center of a flower.

7. Secure the center of the flower with a tiny dab of glue.

8. Separate the floss strands at the center of the flower.

9. Glue two flowers on each side of the ring, just above the ribbons.

Your doll will be a lovely fairy princess when she wears this charming crown.

This jewelry goes in your doll's hair.

Doll Hair Snaps

Here is what you need:

metal snaps about the size of your pinkie nail

ribbon roses

tiny embroidered appliqués

thin craft ribbon

craft jewels

flat shape buttons

scissors

white craft glue

Styrofoam tray to work on

Here is what you do:

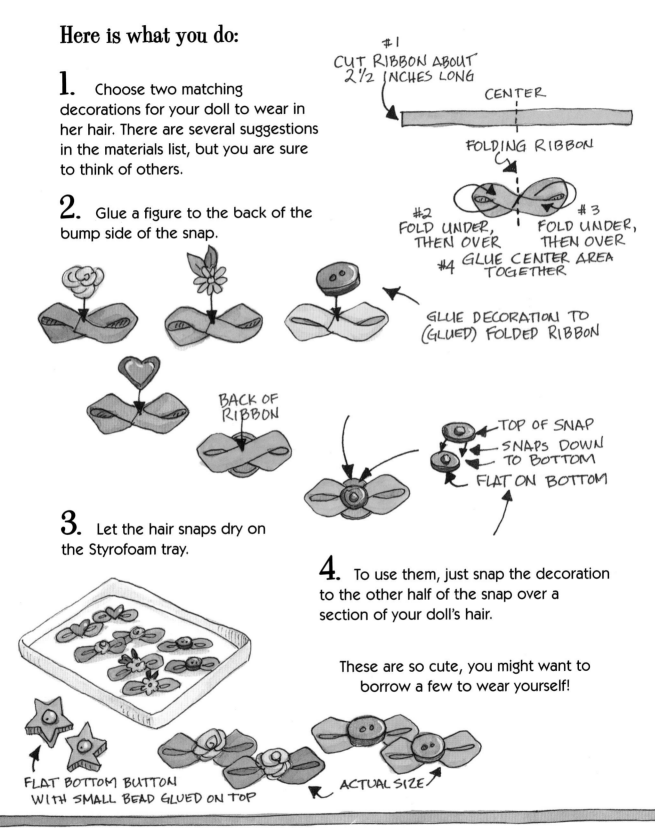

1. Choose two matching decorations for your doll to wear in her hair. There are several suggestions in the materials list, but you are sure to think of others.

2. Glue a figure to the back of the bump side of the snap.

#1
CUT RIBBON ABOUT 2½ INCHES LONG

CENTER

FOLDING RIBBON

#2 FOLD UNDER, THEN OVER

#3 FOLD UNDER, THEN OVER

#4 GLUE CENTER AREA TOGETHER

GLUE DECORATION TO (GLUED) FOLDED RIBBON

BACK OF RIBBON

TOP OF SNAP
SNAPS DOWN TO BOTTOM
FLAT ON BOTTOM

3. Let the hair snaps dry on the Styrofoam tray.

4. To use them, just snap the decoration to the other half of the snap over a section of your doll's hair.

These are so cute, you might want to borrow a few to wear yourself!

FLAT BOTTOM BUTTON WITH SMALL BEAD GLUED ON TOP

ACTUAL SIZE

A perfect gift for your doll—a framed photograph of you!

Doll-Size Picture Frame

Here is what you need:

pretty trim, rickrack, or ribbon

plastic flip-top, like the ones on salad dressing bottles

scissors

school picture or small headshot of you

pencil

white craft glue

Here is what you do:

1. Use the pencil to trace around the opening of the cap on a photo of you. Try to center your head in the traced circle.

2. Cut the photo out on the inside of the traced line.

3. Trim the photo edges as needed to fit the photo inside the plastic cap.

4. Open the flip-top so that the cap stands up like a picture frame.

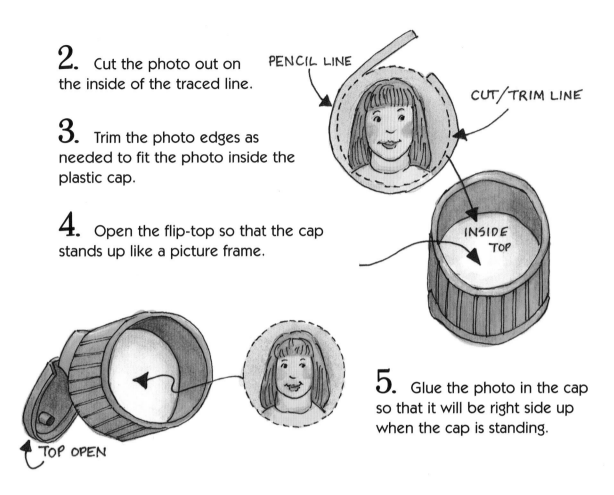

PENCIL LINE

CUT/TRIM LINE

INSIDE TOP

TOP OPEN

5. Glue the photo in the cap so that it will be right side up when the cap is standing.

6. Glue trim around the outside of the bottom portion of the cap (now the front of the frame) to decorate the frame. Make sure that the flip-top is open and you do not get glue on that section of the cap.

Maybe your doll has a very good friend she would like a framed picture of, too. Look in a catalog for your doll or a similar doll to find her some photos of "friends" to frame.

About the Author and Illustrator

Thirty years as a teacher and director of nursery school programs have given Kathy Ross extensive experience in guiding young children through craft projects. Among the more than forty craft books she has written are *Crafts for All Seasons, Kathy Ross Crafts Letter Shapes, All New Crafts for Valentine's Day, Crafts that Celebrate Black History,* and *Play-Doh"! Fun and Games.* To find out more about Kathy, visit her Web site: www.Kathyross.com.

Elaine Garvin designs and illustrates greeting cards, and she has illustrated more than twenty children's books over the past ten years. A member of the Society of Children's Book Writers and Illustrators and the Graphic Artists Guild, she lives and works in Massachusetts.